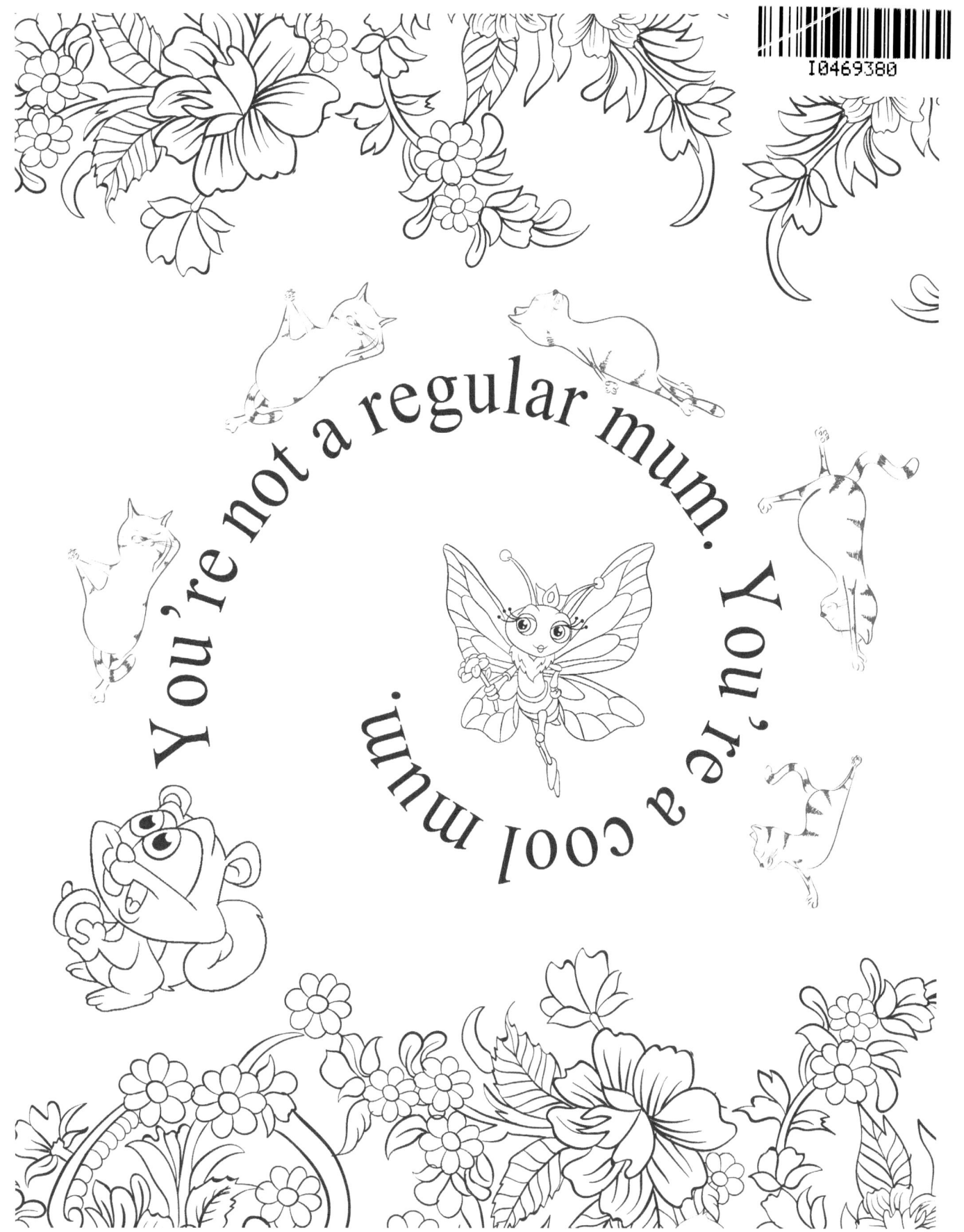

You're not a regular mum. You're a cool mum.

Illustrated by:
Mandala & Caricature Illustration
Joshua Lazana Lagman and Jade Villaremo

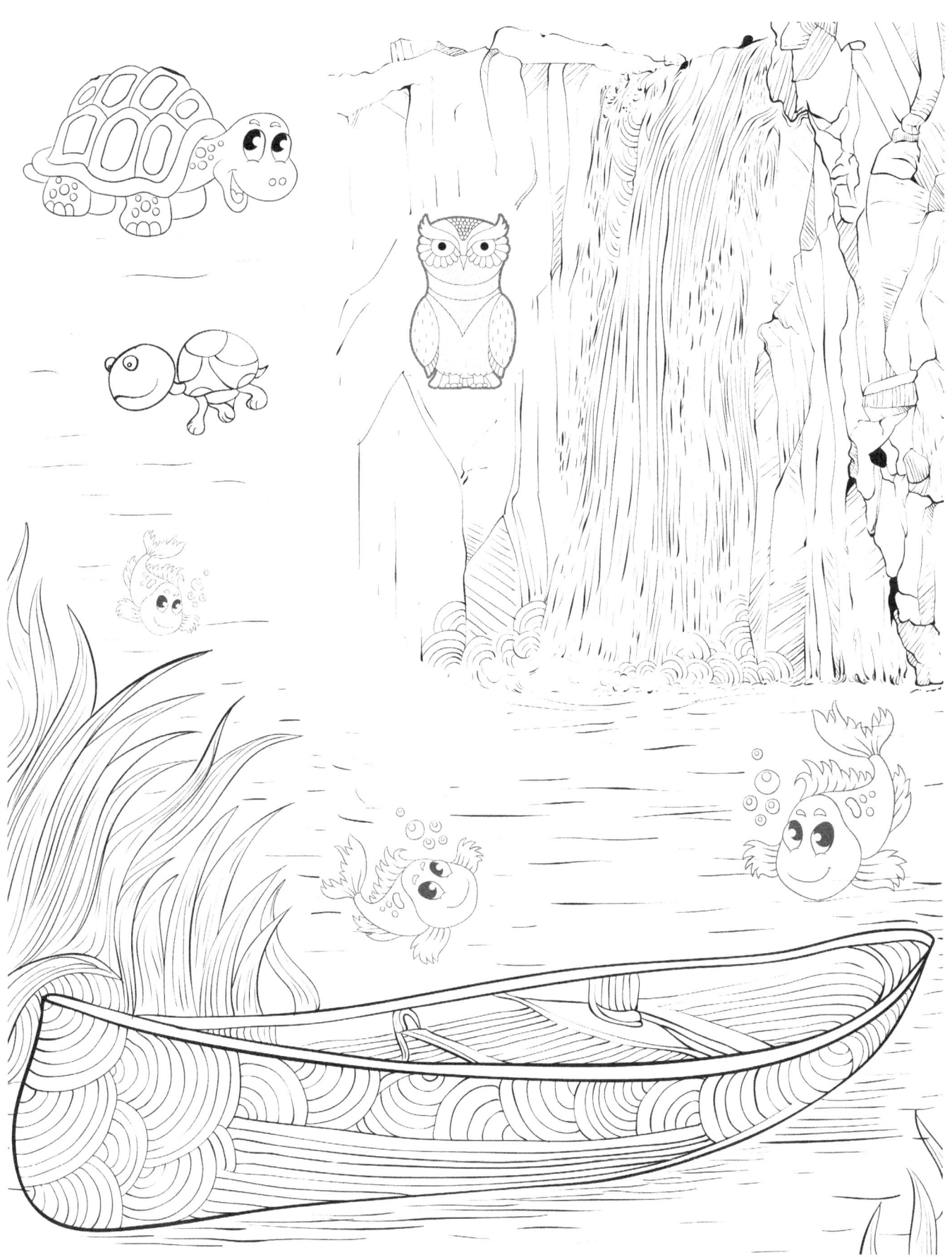

A MOTHER IS LIKE A FLOWER. EACH ONE IS BEAUTIFUL AND UNIQUE.

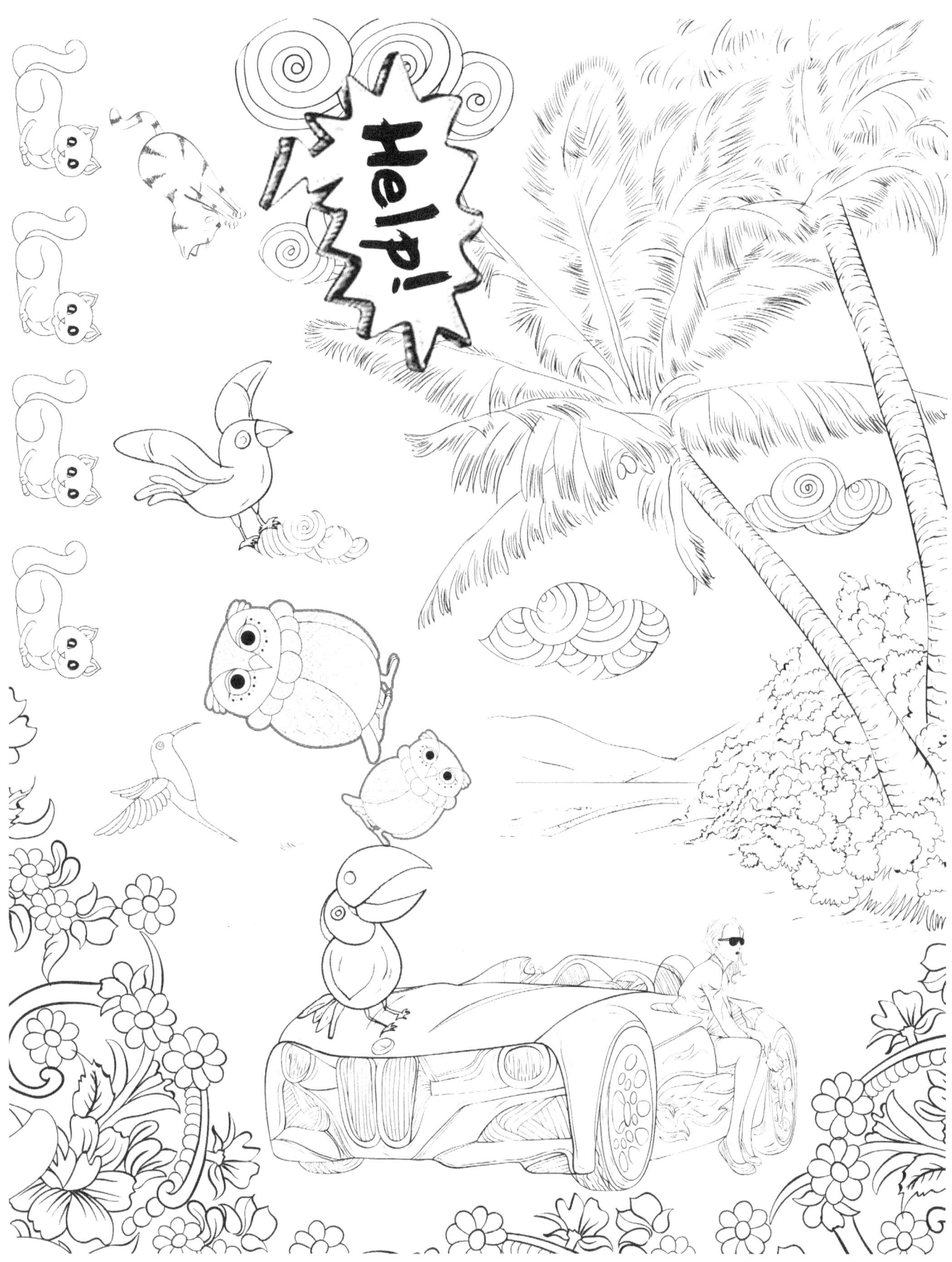

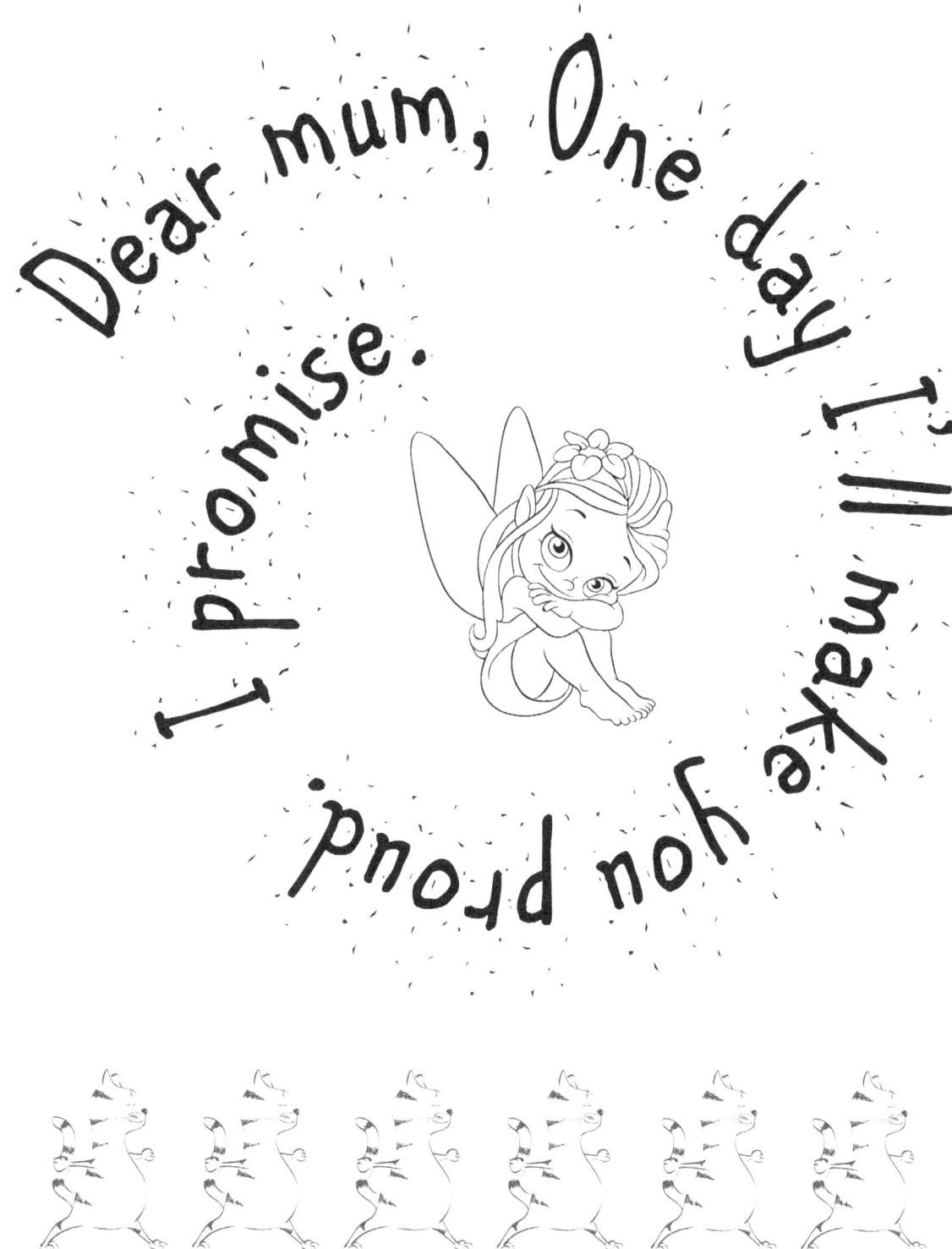

Dear mum, One day I'll make you proud. I promise.

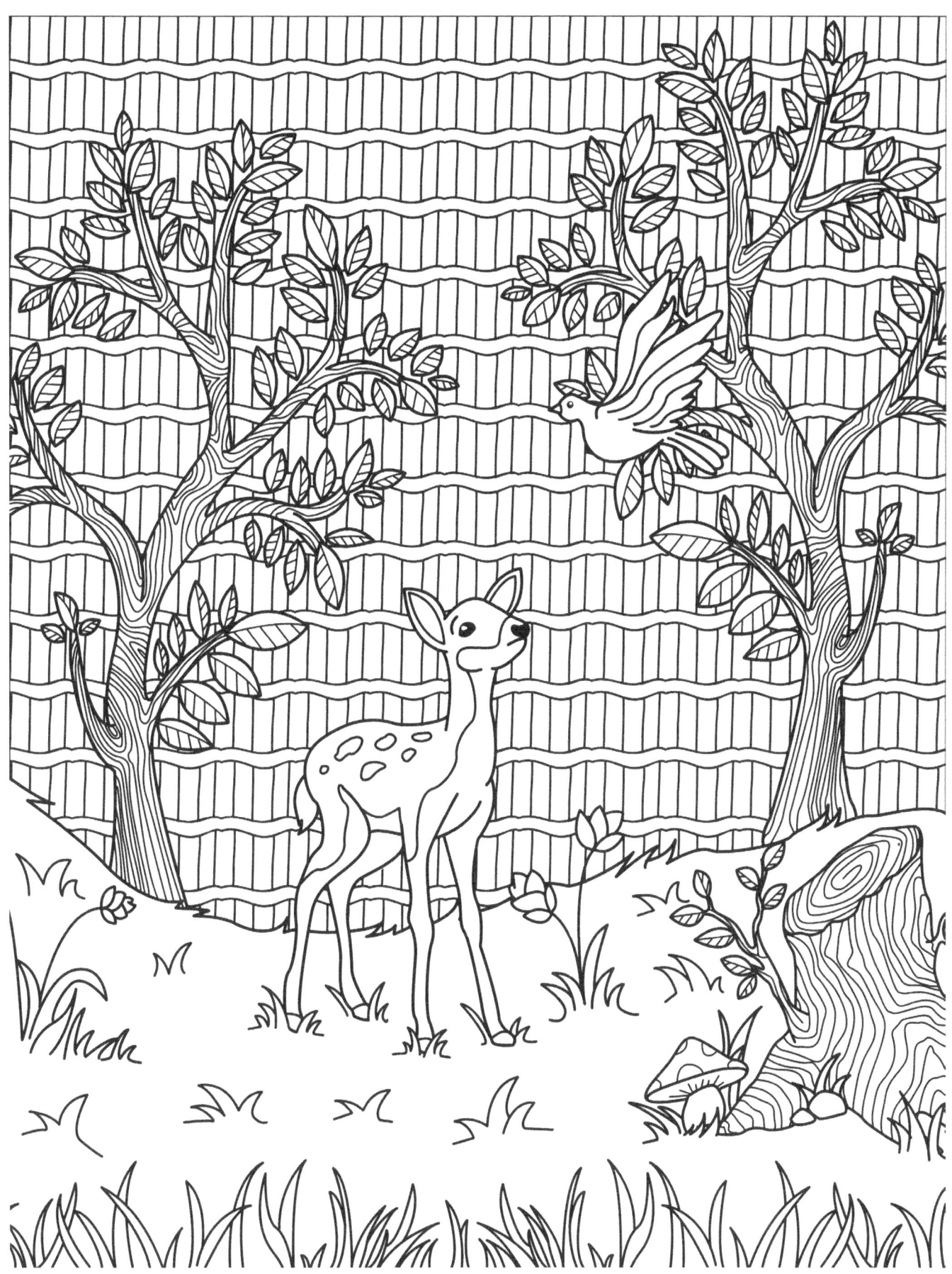

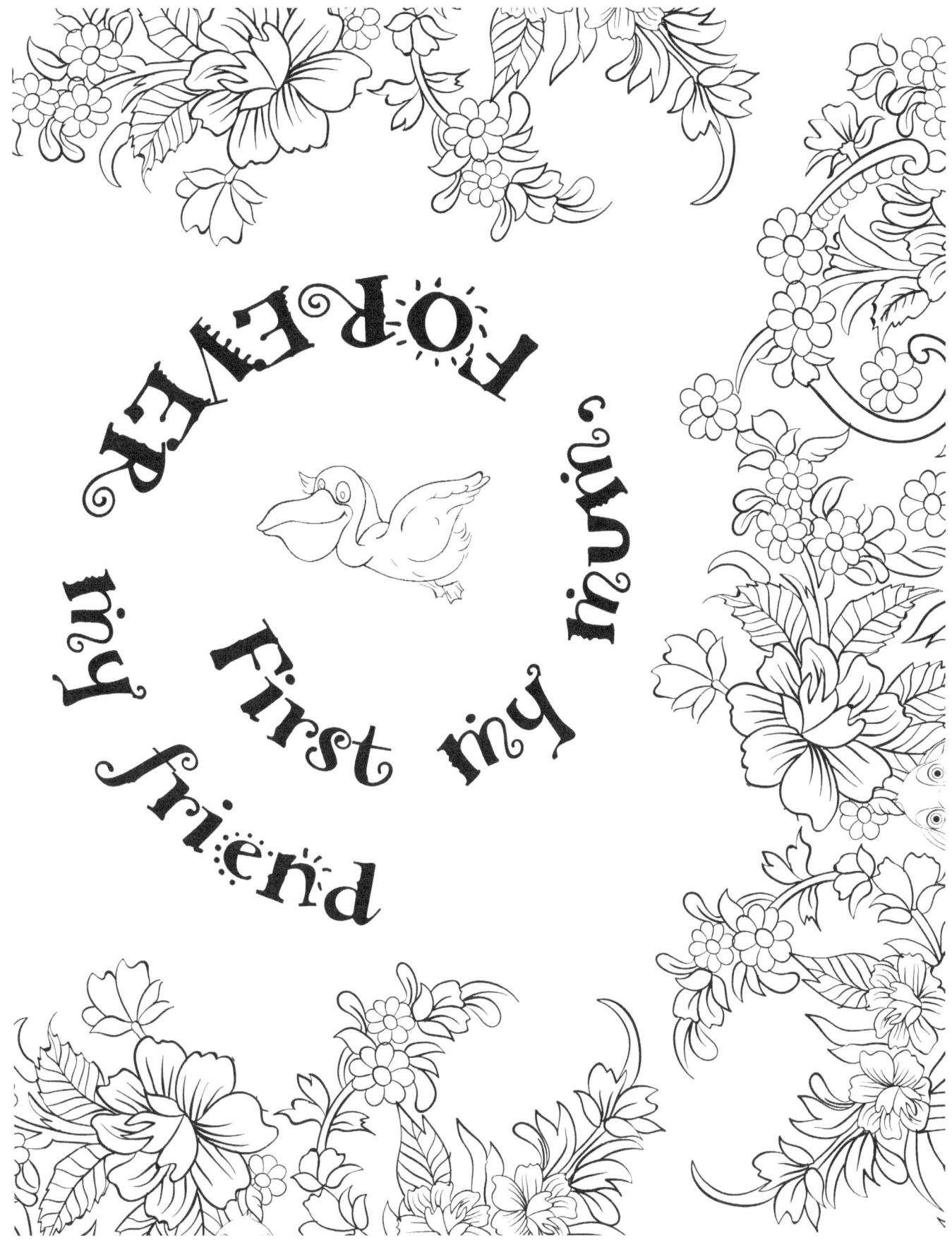

FOREVER

First my mum,
my friend
my

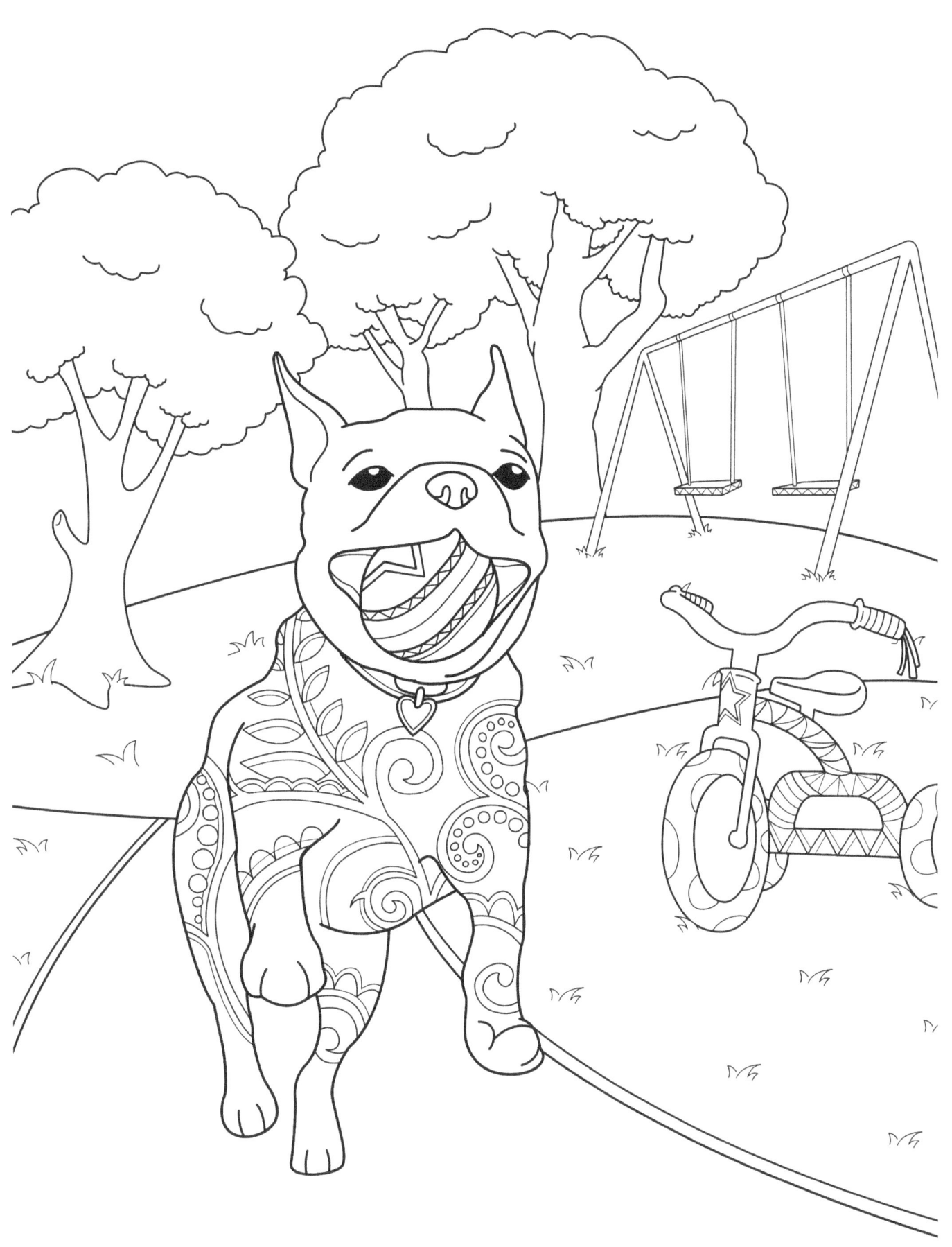

The more I grow, the more I realize that my mum is the best best best friend that I ever had.

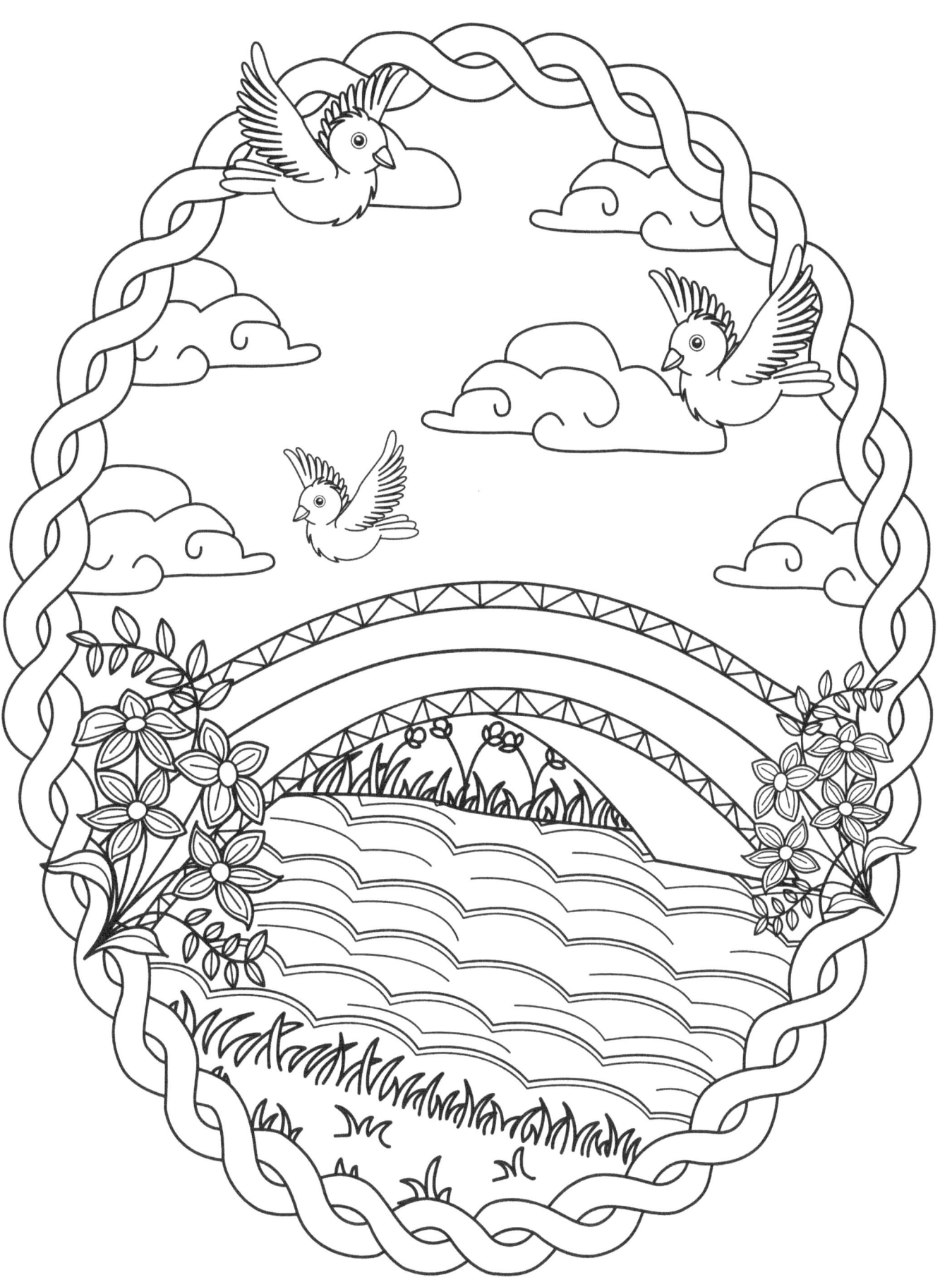

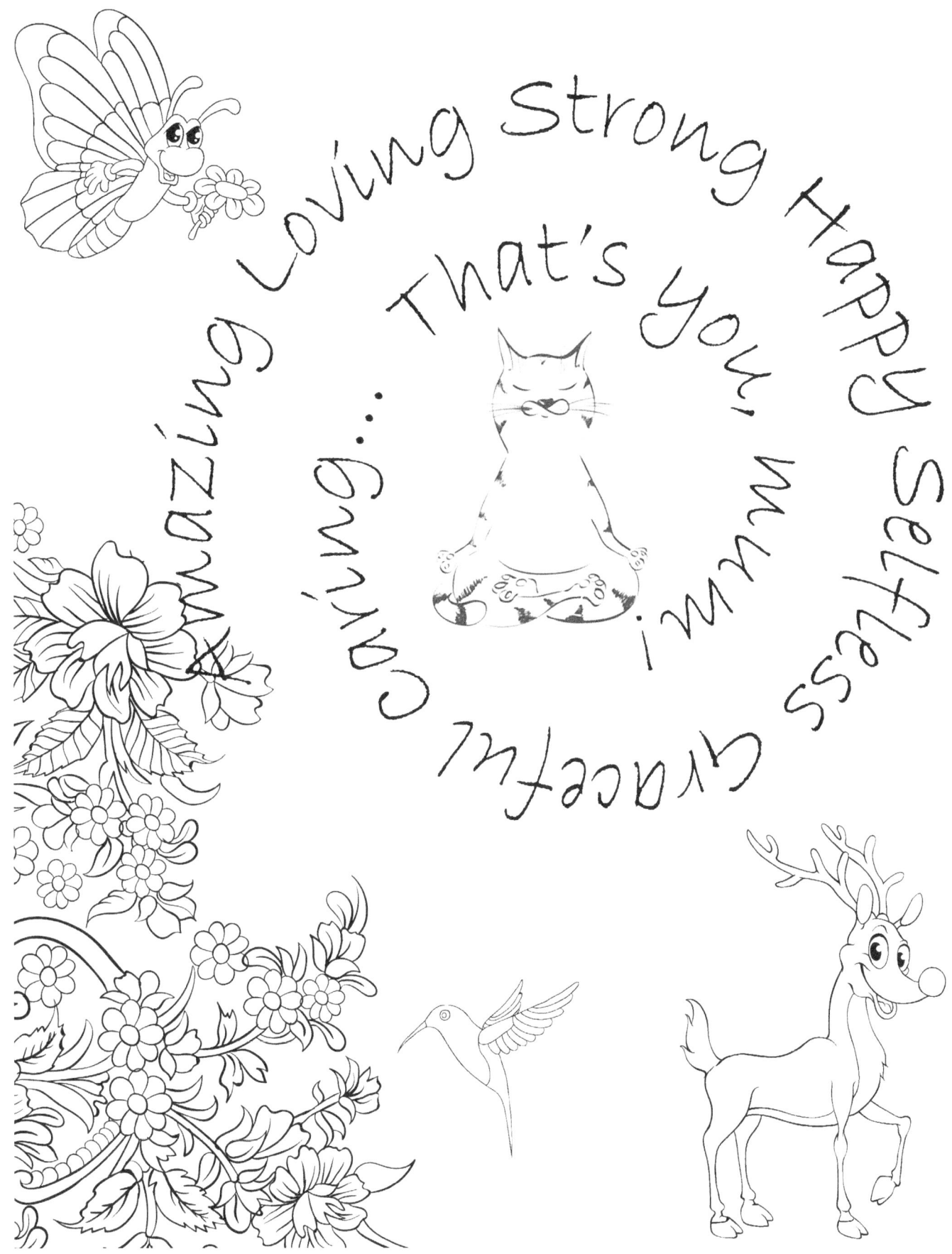

Amazing Loving Strong Happy Selfless Graceful caring... That's you, mum!

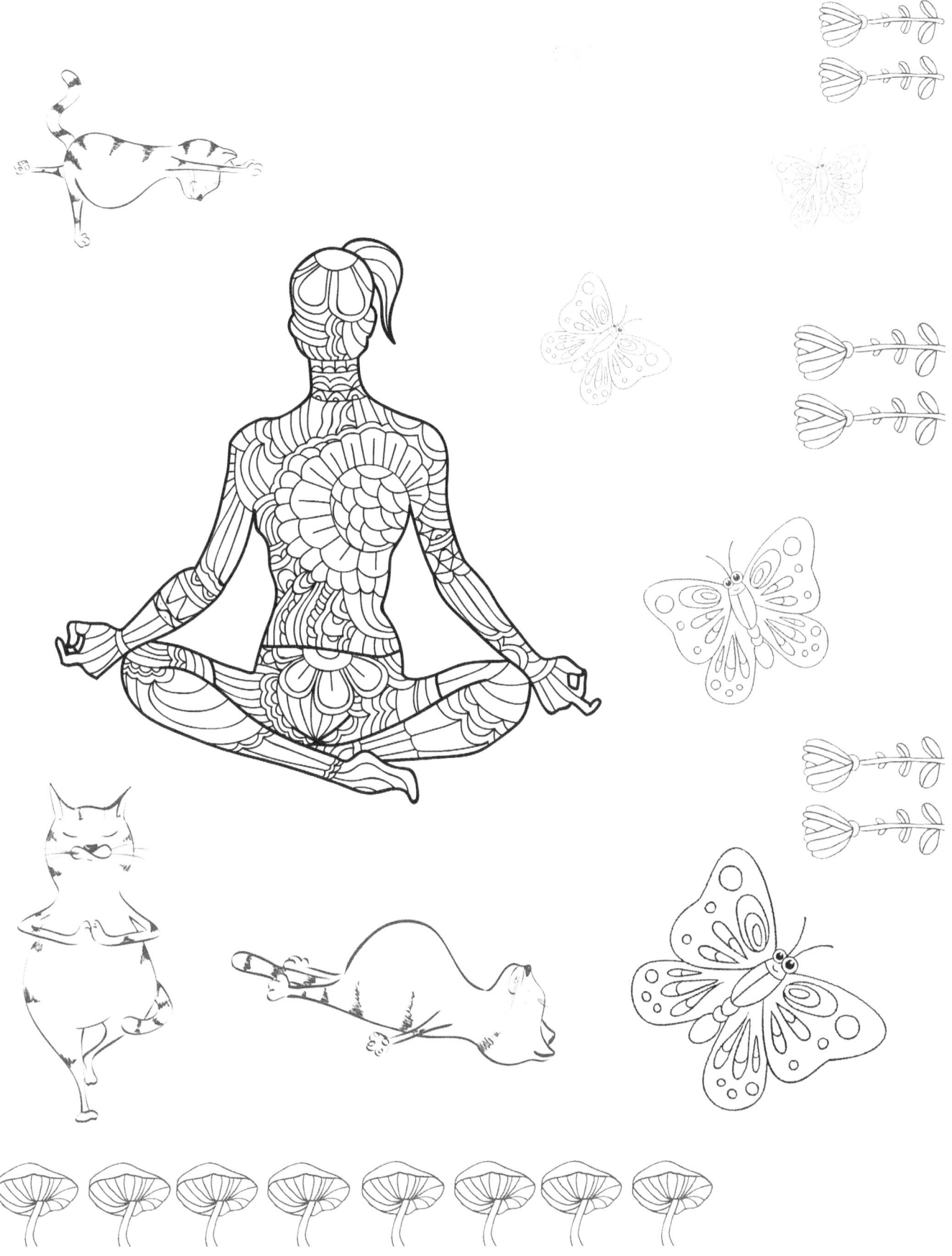

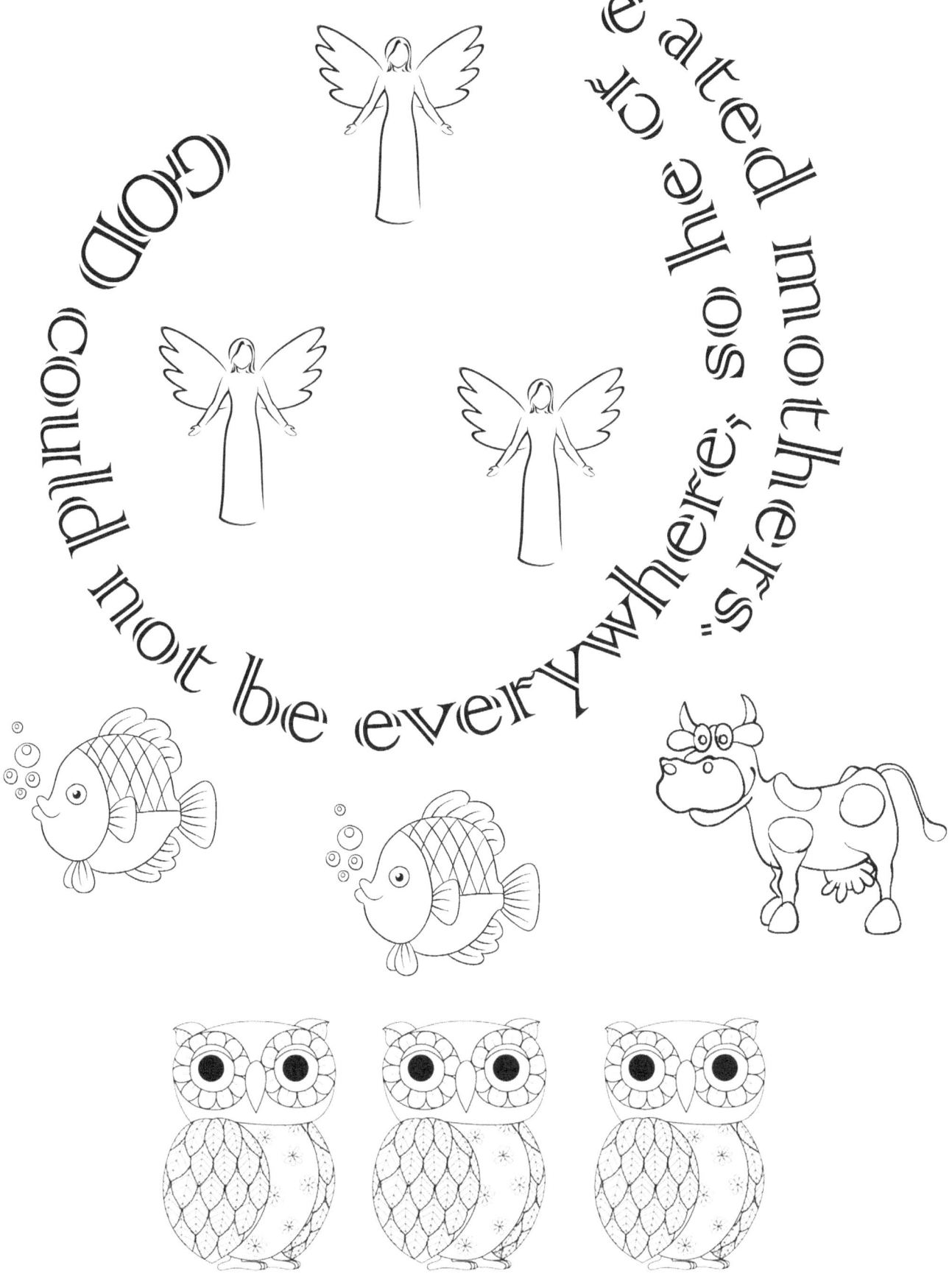

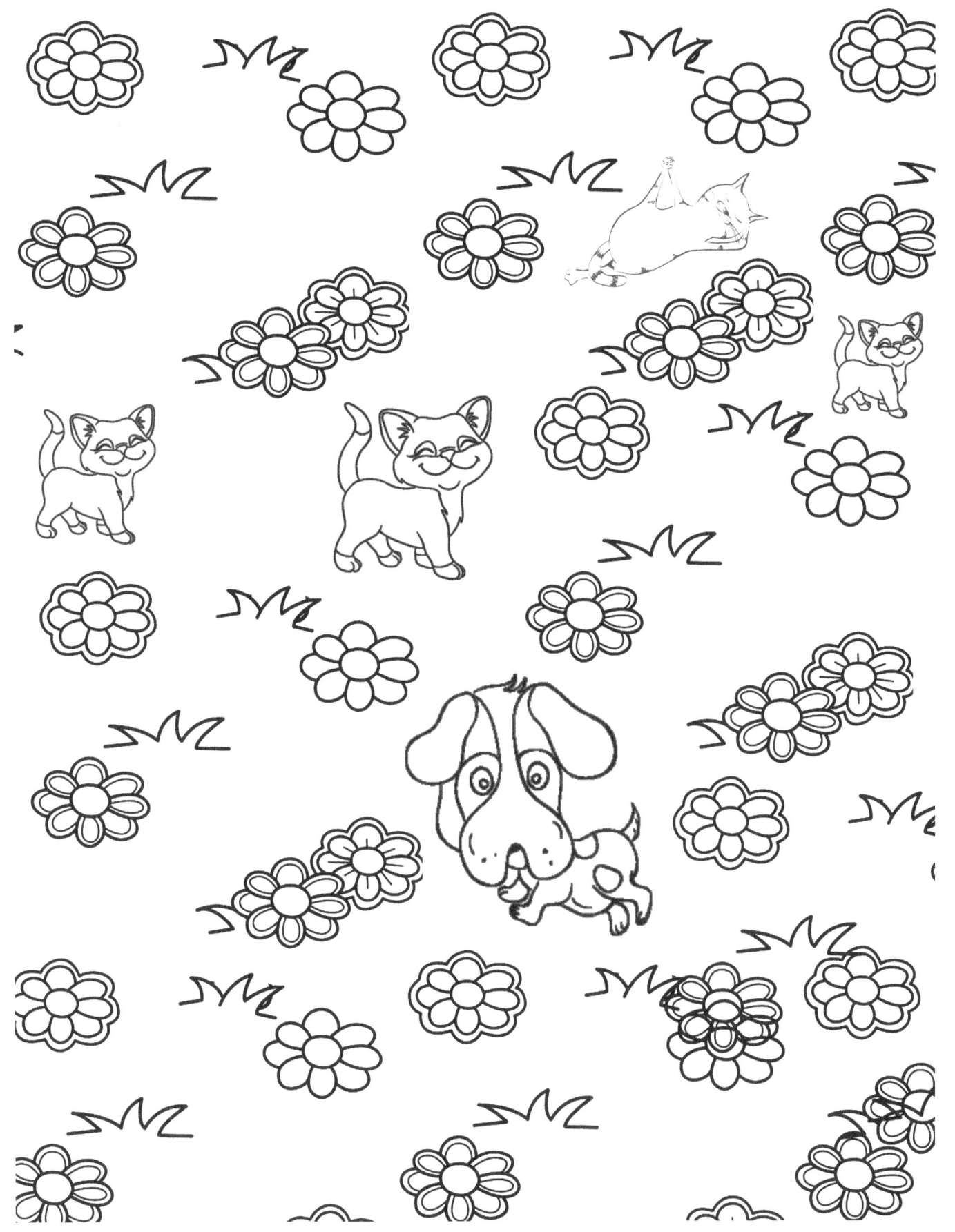

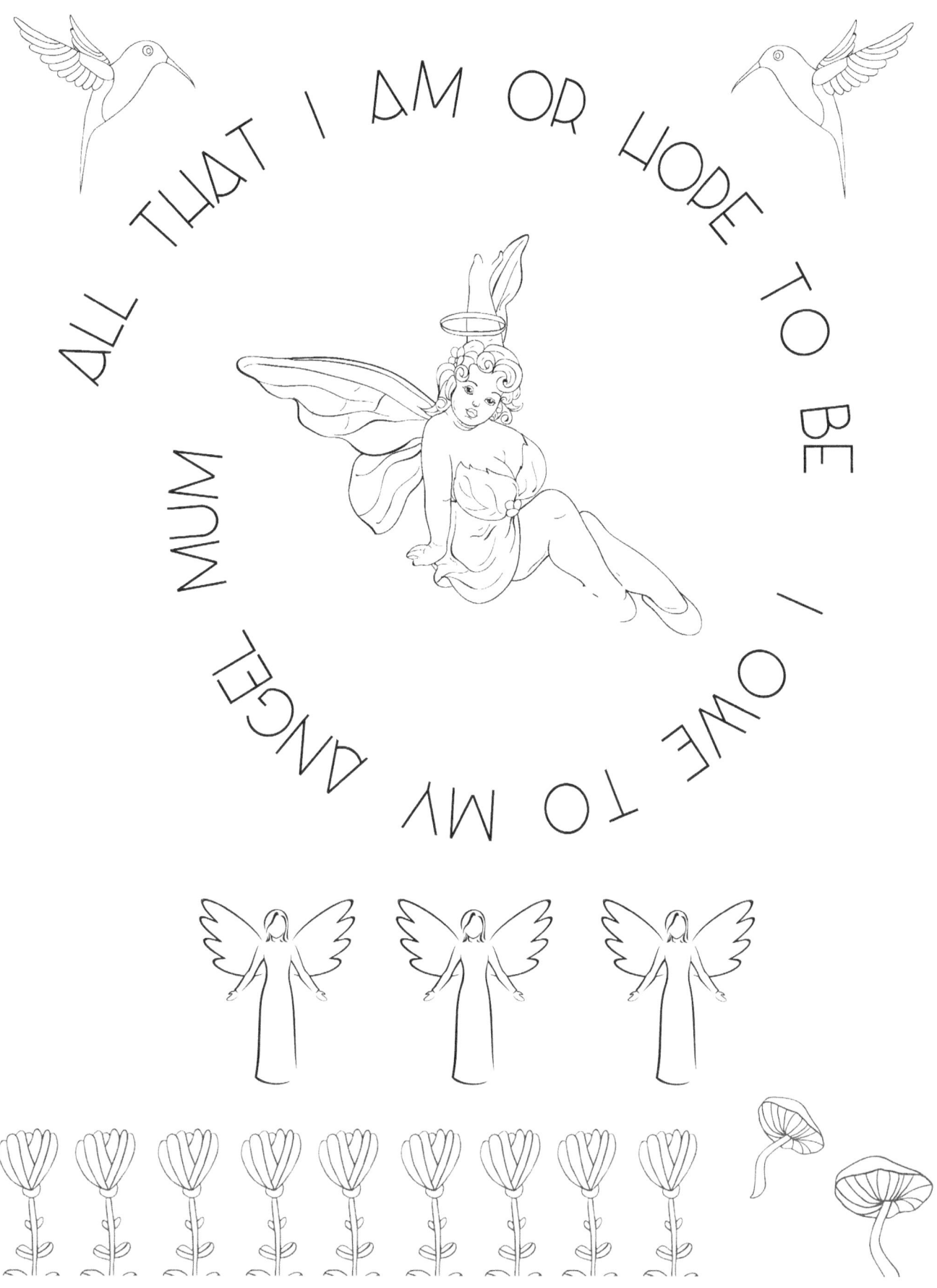

ALL THAT I AM OR HOPE TO BE I OWE TO MY ANGEL MUM

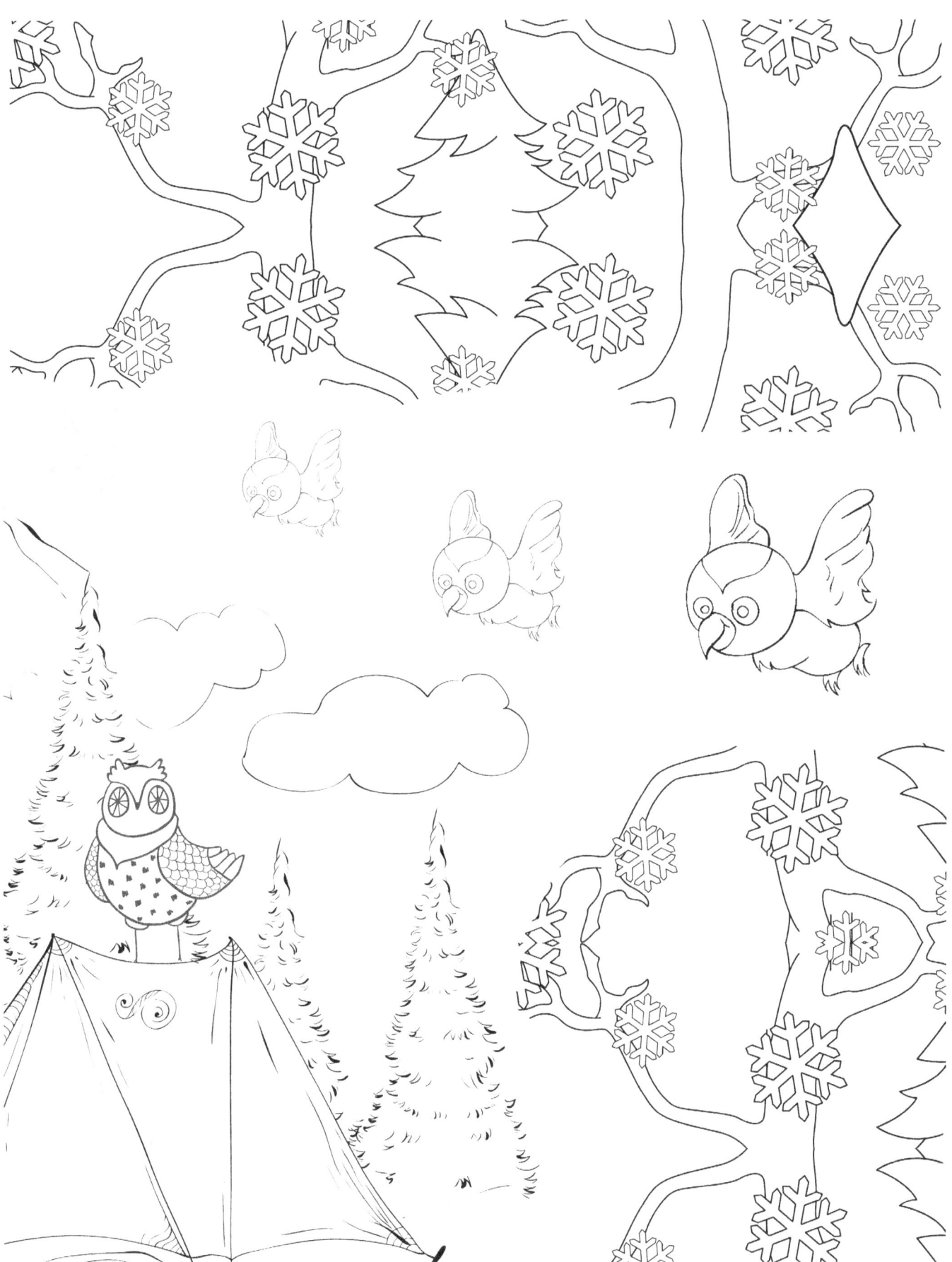

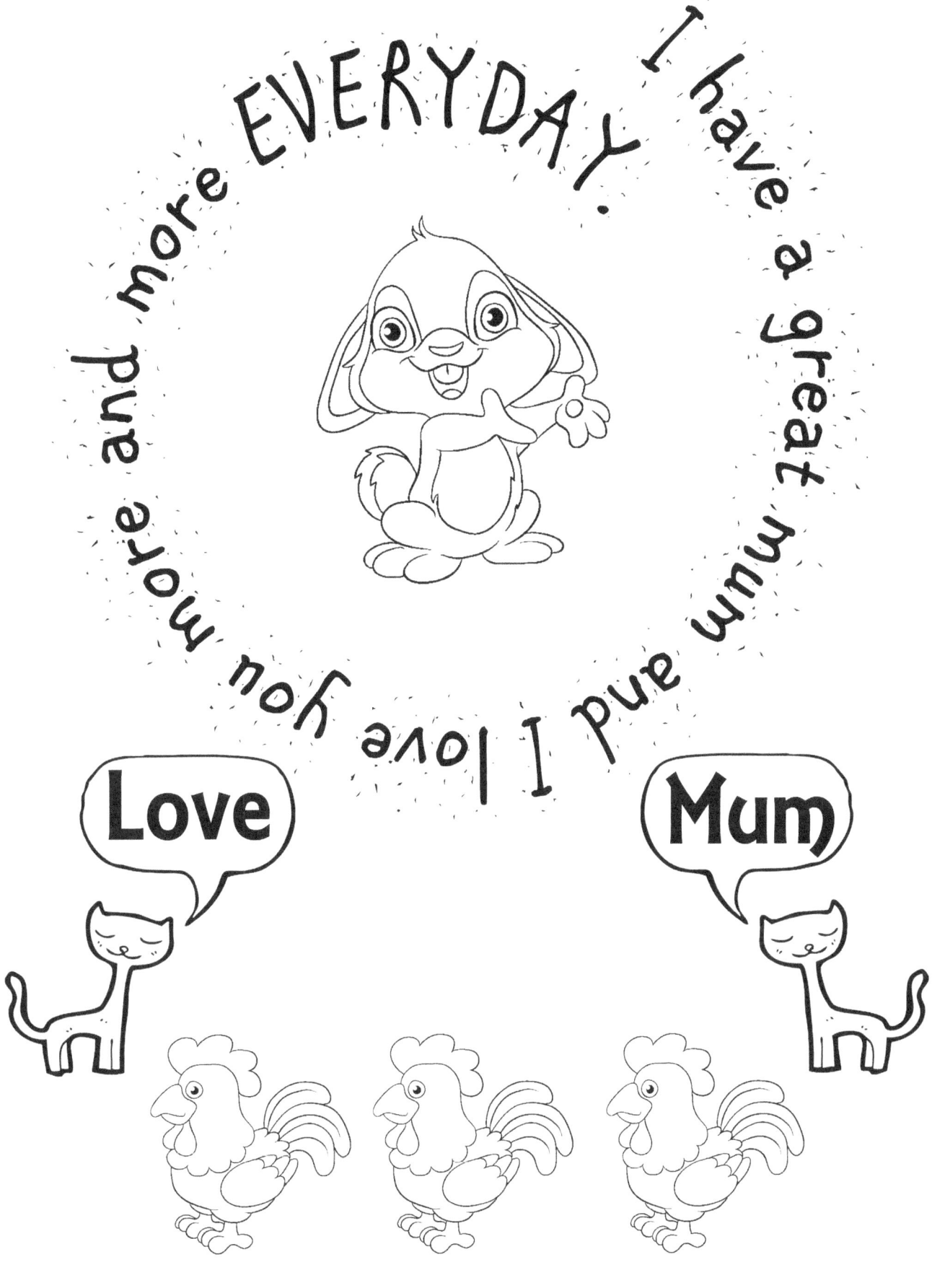

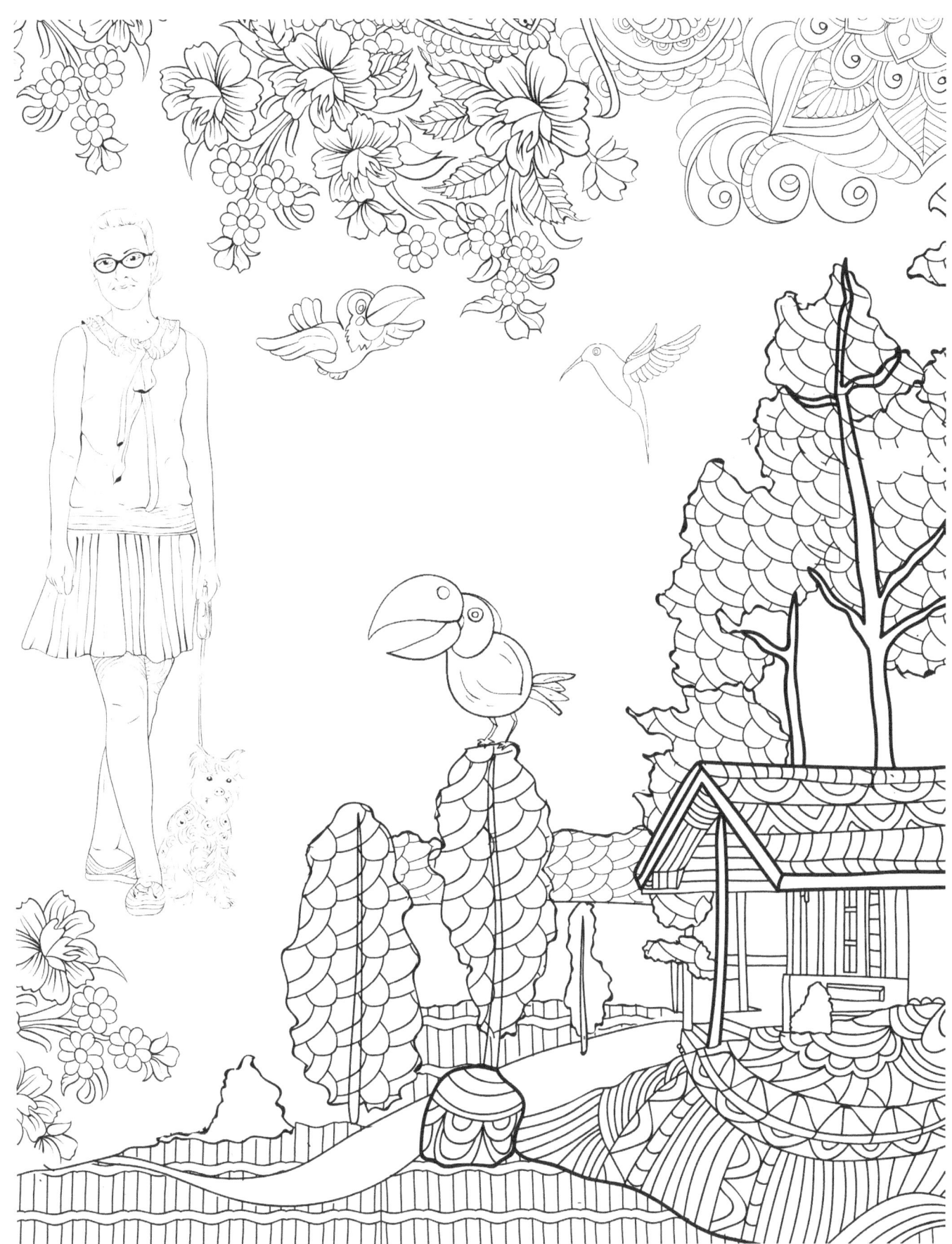

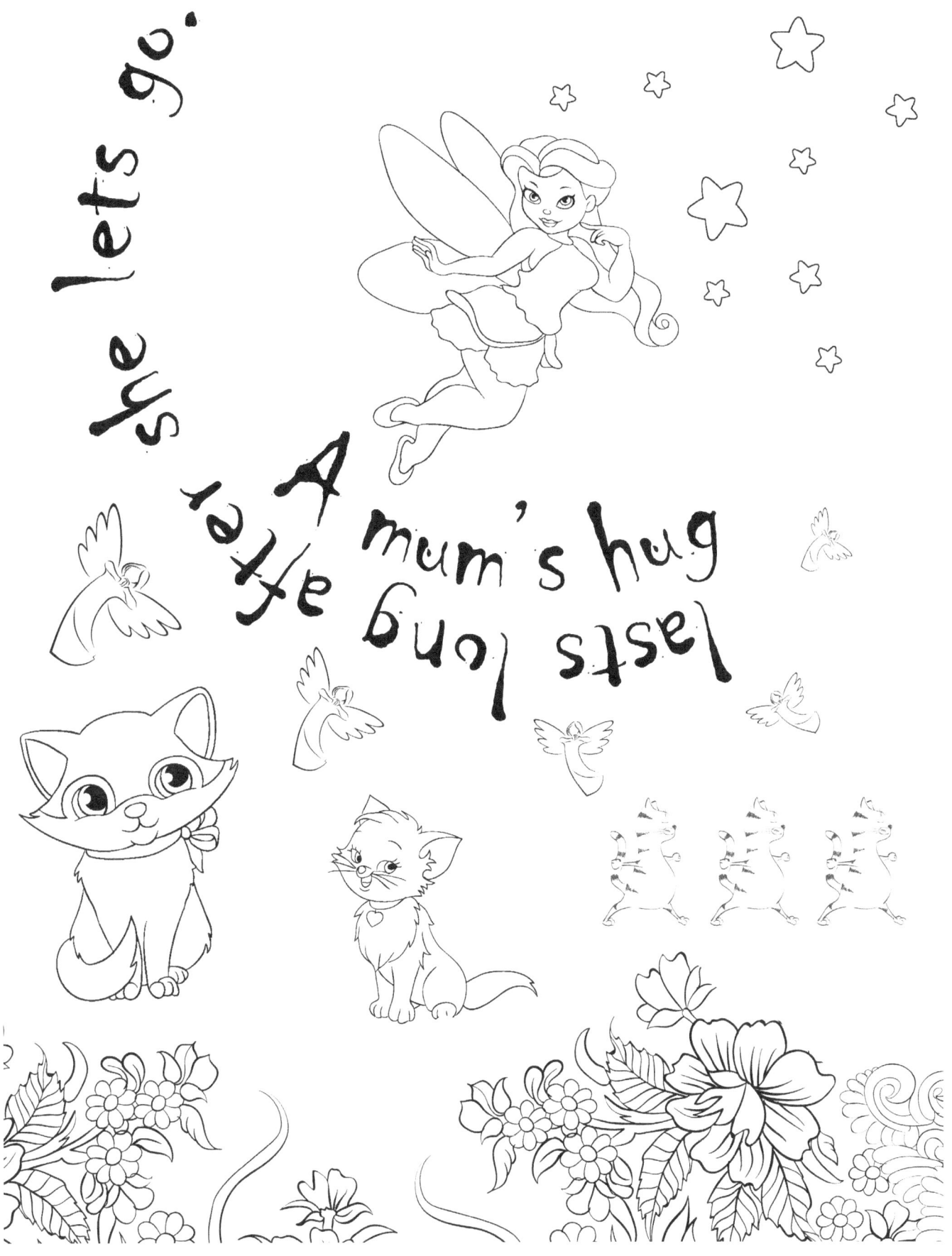

A mum's hug lasts long after she lets go.

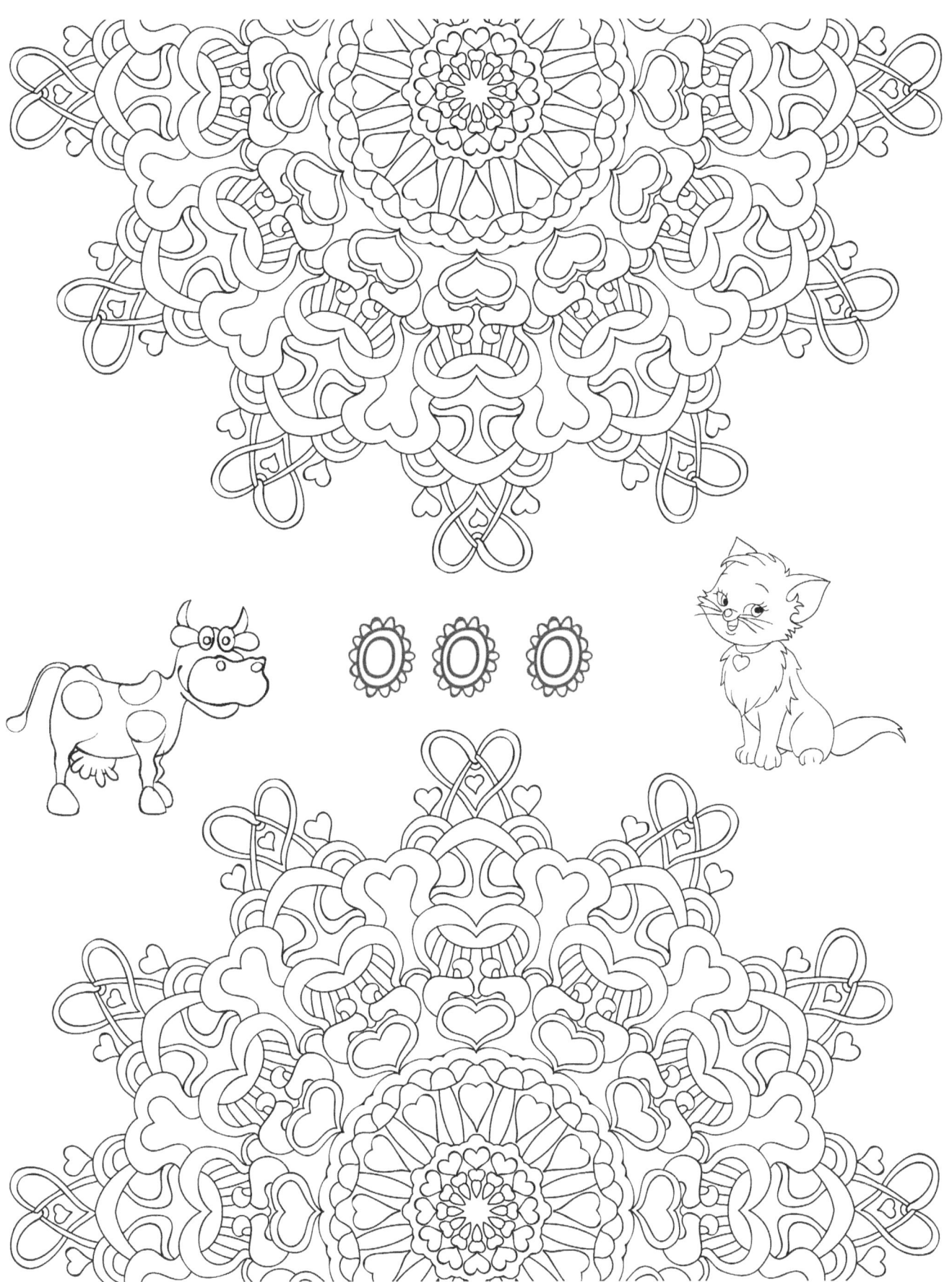

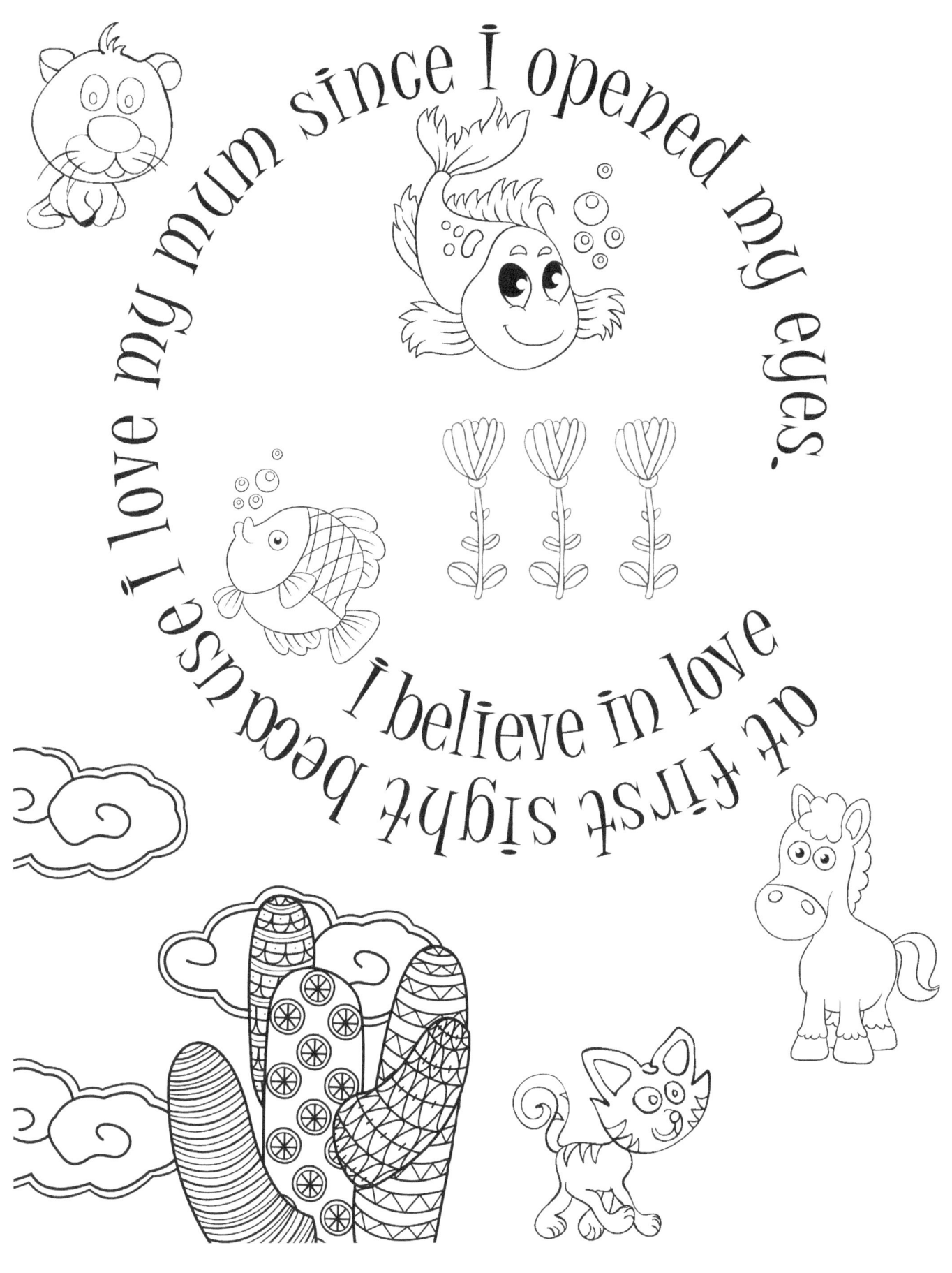

I love my mum since I opened my eyes. I believe in love at first sight because I love my mum.

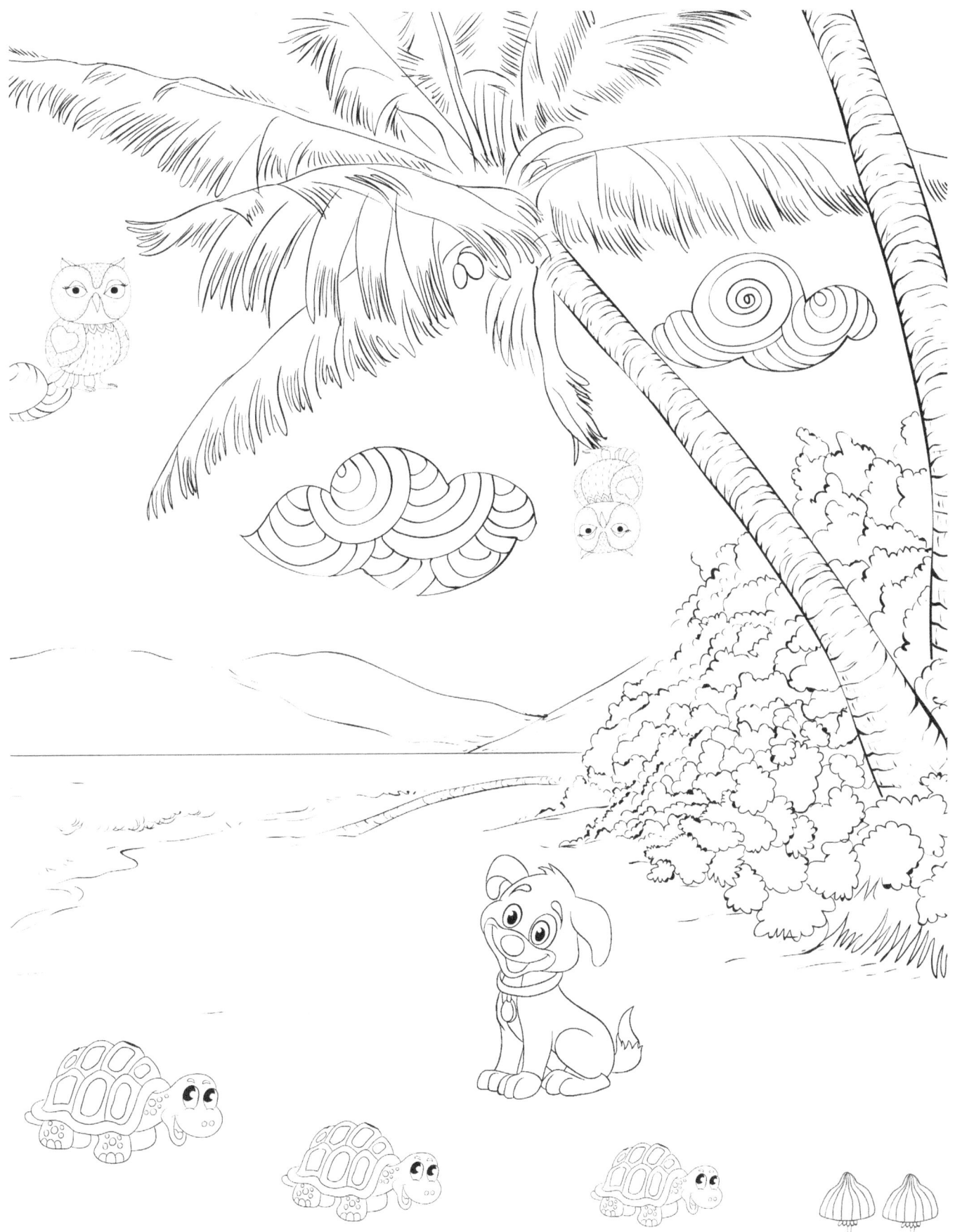

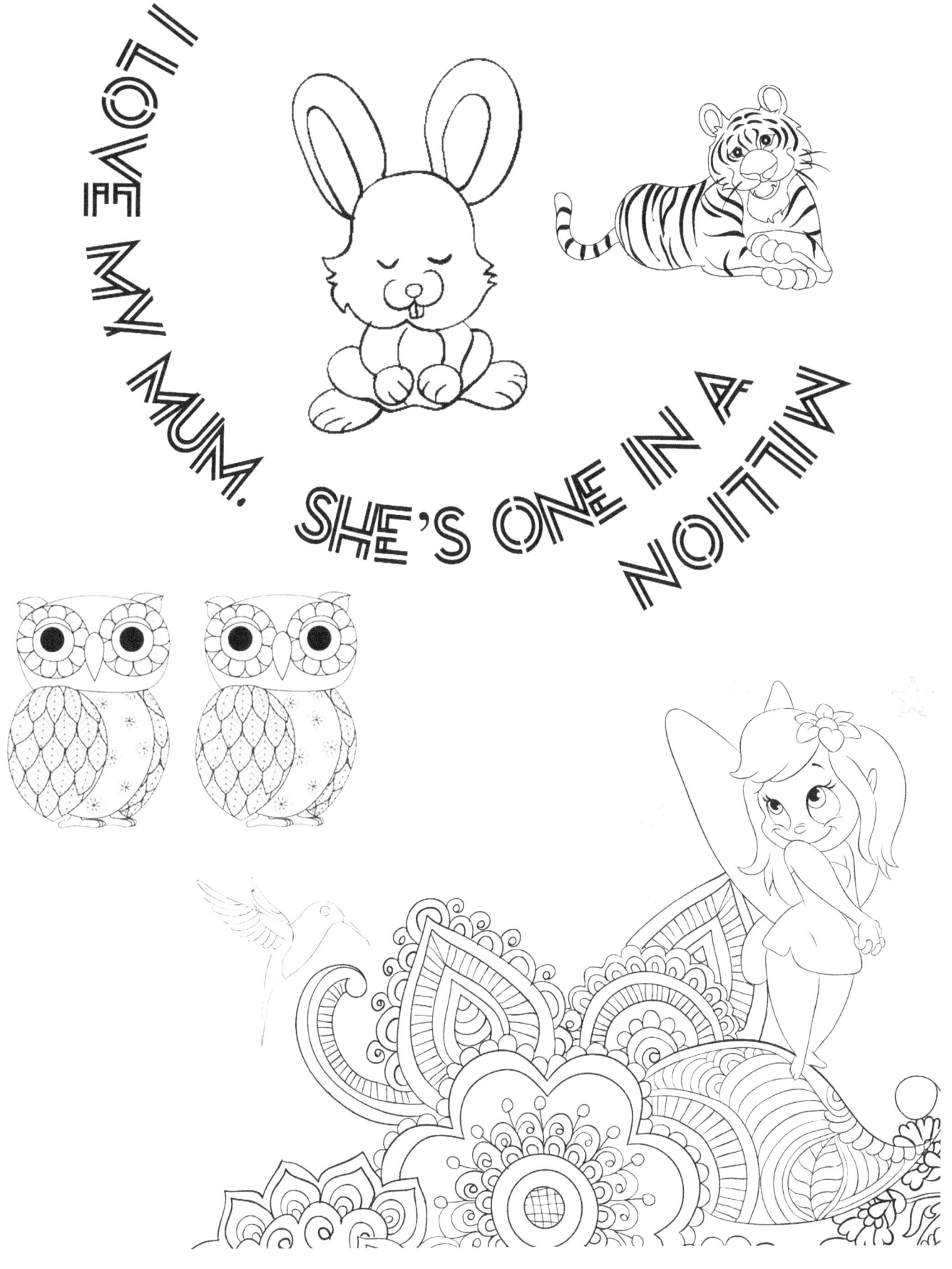

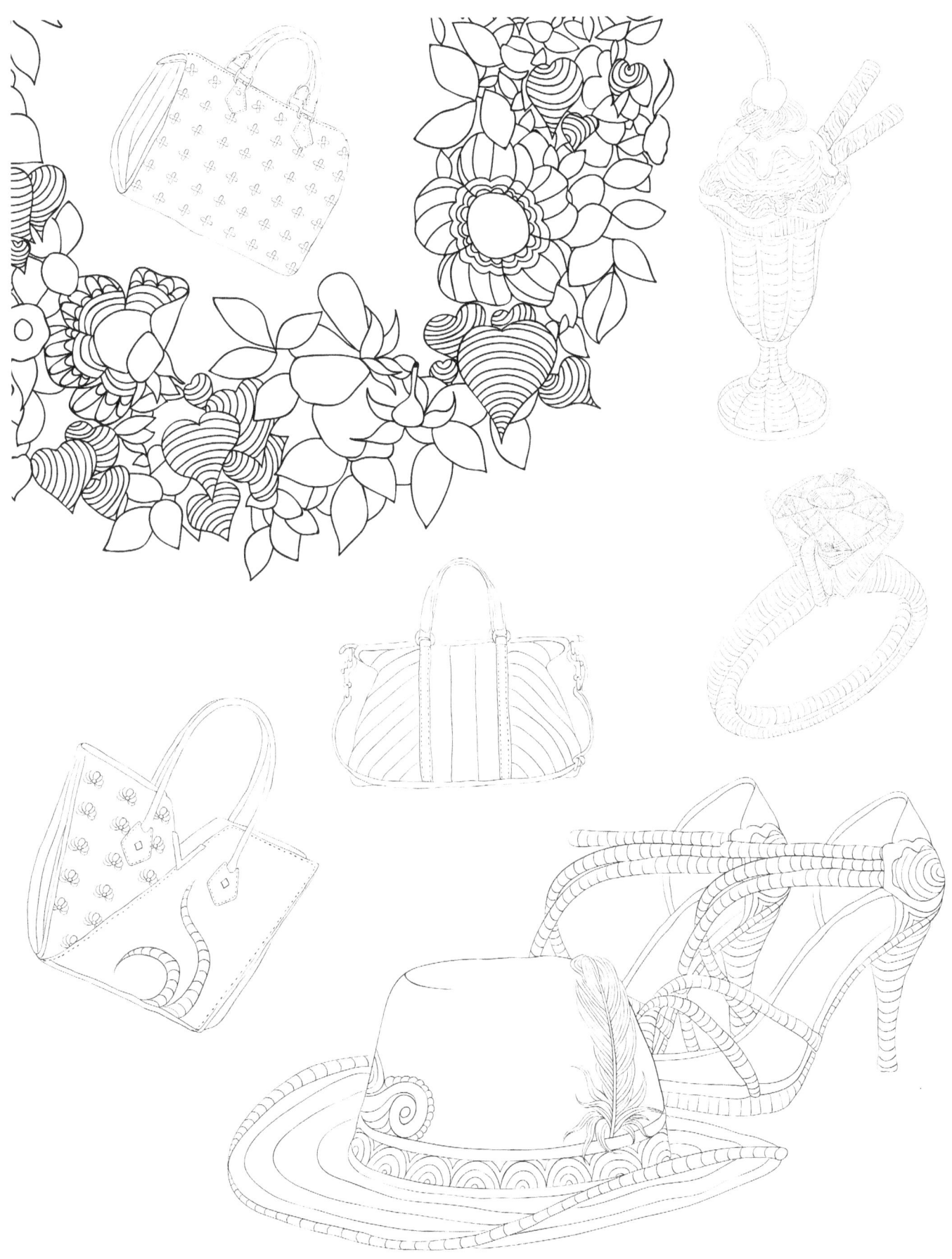

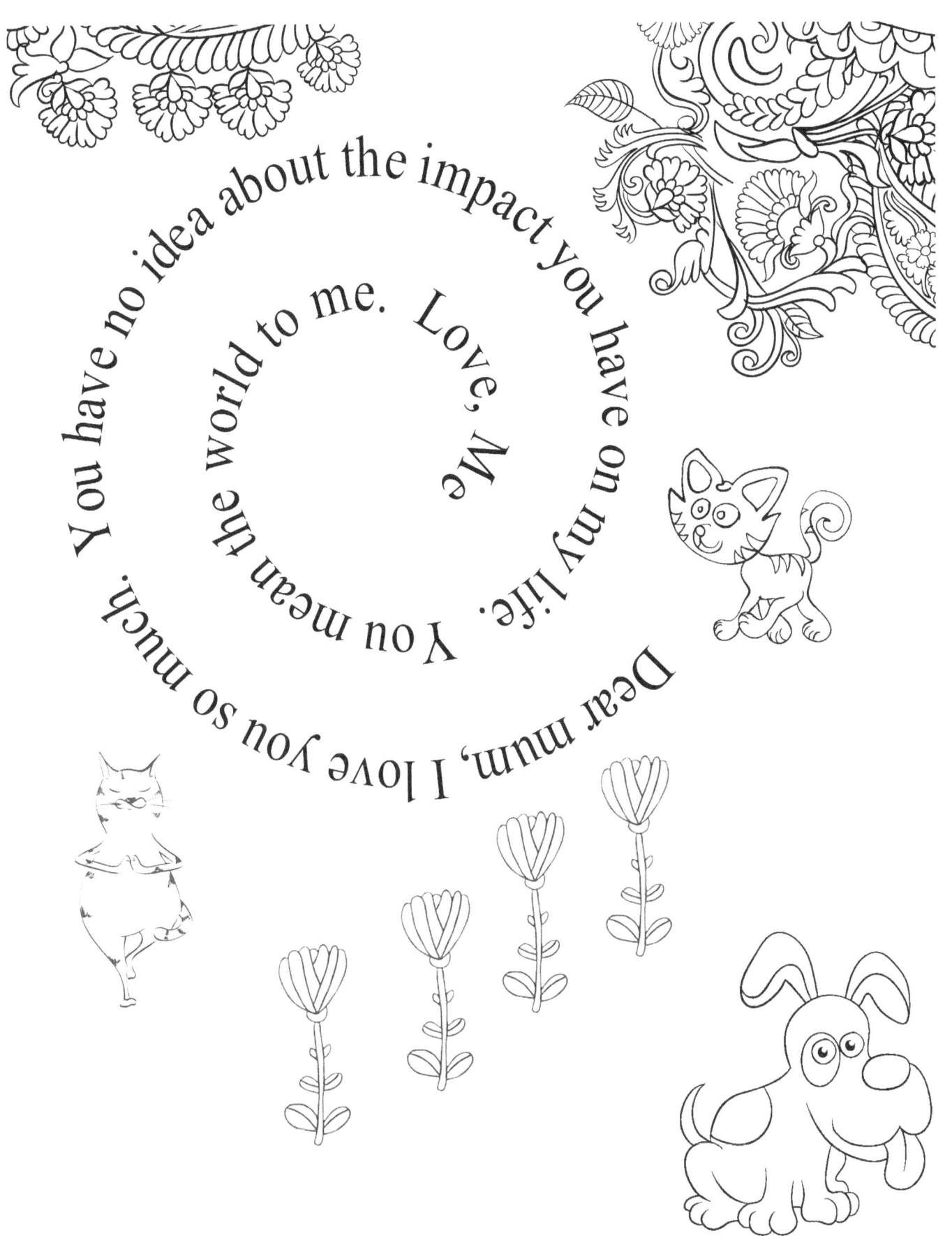

Dear mum, I love you so much. You mean the world to me. You have no idea about the impact you have on my life. You have no idea about the impact you have on my life. Love, Me